AWAKENING THE NEW

HUMAN REVOLUTION

I0558695

From Survival to Conscious Creation

Dr. W. Koros

For every reader who dares to journey inward.

ACKNOWLEDGEMENT

With gratitude to my family, mentors, and readers, your quiet strength, encouragement, and belief continue to make these words possible.

CONTENTS

INTRODUCTION – THE EDGE OF TRANSFORMATION

Every age of humanity has its thresholds — moments when the familiar story begins to fray, when the structures we thought unshakable tremble, when the future yawns wide with both danger and promise. We are living in such a moment now.

Around us, the world appears both dazzling and fragile. Technological marvels make life faster and more interconnected than ever before. A message can circle the globe in seconds. Satellites map the Earth with exquisite precision. Artificial intelligence assists with medical diagnoses, scientific research, and even the arts. Yet, alongside this progress, the human story is marked by fractures: ecological breakdown, political polarization, and the silent epidemics of loneliness and despair.

It feels, at times, as though we are racing forward and falling apart all at once.

But history reminds us that moments of upheaval are also moments of profound possibility. The agricultural revolution transformed small bands of hunter-gatherers into the architects of cities. The Renaissance reawakened creativity and human dignity after centuries of darkness. The industrial revolution reshaped economies and societies, pulling millions from subsistence into modernity.

Each of these shifts carried both light and shadow. Agriculture gave abundance, but also hierarchy. Industry brought wealth but also exploitation. Technology connected us, but also isolated us. What has been missing in every past revolution is the conscious shaping of who we are as humans at the center of the change.

That is the challenge of our time. The question is no longer only what we can do, but who we are becoming.

We stand at the edge of what I call the New Human Revolution — not a revolution of weapons or ideology, but of consciousness. It is a revolution that asks us to evolve beyond the instincts of fear and scarcity, beyond the stories of division and domination, into a new way of perceiving ourselves and our place in the world.

This revolution does not belong to governments or corporations alone. It belongs to each of us. It begins in our daily choices — in how we see, how we relate, how we create. And it extends outward into communities, nations, and the planet itself.

The chapters that follow are not meant to predict the future in detail. No one can. Instead, they invite us to recognize the seeds of transformation already sprouting within us and around us, and to nurture them into full bloom. They invite us to participate in writing a new story — one where survival is no longer the highest goal, but the starting point for a flourishing humanity.

The New Human Revolution has already begun. The question is: will you step into it?

CHAPTER 1 – THE OLD HUMAN STORY

To understand the urgency of this new revolution, we must first look unflinchingly at the story that has carried humanity until now. This is the old human story — the narrative of survival, competition, and domination that has shaped our cultures, our economies, and our inner lives for millennia.

In the beginning, this story was not a failure but a necessity. Early humans faced a harsh world. Survival demanded vigilance: Who is friend? Who is foe? Where is food? Where is danger? Our nervous systems evolved to react quickly, to fight or flee, to guard our tribes and hoard our resources. Fear was not weakness; it was a form of intelligence that kept us alive.

But what began as adaptation hardened into identity. The instinct to protect grew into a habit of conquest. Tribes expanded into empires, competing for land, wealth, and power. Survival logic became empire logic: if we do not dominate, we will be dominated. The old story gave rise to armies, borders, hierarchies, and entire civilizations built on the principle that someone must lose for someone else to win.

This story is etched into the milestones of history. The agricultural revolution brought abundance but also systems of ownership and control. The industrial revolution multiplied wealth but also widened inequality and stripped the Earth. Political revolutions promised freedom, but often replaced one ruling class with another.

We have called these eras "progress," and in many ways, they were. They lifted millions from hunger, brought scientific breakthroughs, and birthed art and philosophy of extraordinary depth. But each was incomplete, because each expanded our power without equally expanding our consciousness. We built bigger machines, stronger weapons, taller towers — but rarely asked: What kind of human is wielding this power?

The old story is not confined to history books. It lives in us today. We see it in the executive who sacrifices health and family to climb the corporate ladder, in the politician who stirs division for votes, in communities fractured by fear of difference. The same survival logic — "me versus you," "us versus them," "more for me, less for you" — animates much of our personal and collective life.

And this story has brought us to the brink. We face climate collapse, growing inequality, and technologies capable of immense harm. The old logic, once a tool for survival, now threatens the very survival of the species it once served.

To step forward, we must craft a new story, not by denying our past, but by transcending it. Humanity cannot remain defined solely by fear, consumption, and competition. The old human story has carried us far — but it cannot carry us further.

It is time to write a new one.

CHAPTER 2 – THE SEEDS OF THE

NEW HUMAN

Every revolution begins as a whisper. Long before the banners, the marches, or the declarations of change, there are faint signals that a new story is being written. The New Human Revolution is no different. Its beginnings are subtle, sometimes so quiet that they are overlooked — yet they are here, already taking root in the cracks of a weary world.

Some of these seeds are biological. For centuries, science believed the brain to be largely fixed after childhood, its pathways locked in by habit. But modern neuroscience has rewritten this assumption. We now know that the human brain is plastic — capable of rewiring, adapting, and expanding throughout life. This means that we are not condemned to repeat the cycles of violence, fear, and prejudice we inherited. Compassion and empathy are not abstract ideals; they are trainable capacities. When a person practices gratitude daily, the brain's neural pathways change.

When children are taught emotional awareness in schools, studies show they become more resilient and empathetic adults. Biology itself whispers that the human being is still unfolding, still becoming.

Other seeds are cultural. Ancient traditions that once seemed archaic are being rediscovered with urgency. Indigenous wisdom, dismissed for centuries as "primitive," is now being recognized as essential knowledge for living in balance with the Earth. In Australia, Aboriginal fire practices are being reintroduced to prevent devastating bushfires, offering lessons in humility and cooperation with nature. In the Amazon, tribes who steward the rainforest remind the world that land is not property but kin. Eastern practices like yoga and meditation, once confined to monasteries, are now embraced globally — not as exotic curiosities but as medicine for restless modern lives. What once was marginalized now rises as a guide for survival.

Seeds of the New Human are also personal and lived. They are seen in ordinary people acting in extraordinary ways. In Rwanda, after the genocide, communities of survivors and perpetrators gather in circles of reconciliation, choosing forgiveness over vengeance. In Japan, elderly volunteers offered to work in the Fukushima nuclear zone after the disaster, preferring to risk their own health to spare younger generations. In small towns across the world, neighbors create gardens to feed the hungry, build shelters for the homeless, or stand together against injustice. These acts may not make global headlines, but they are the heartbeat of a new human story.

And then there are the seeds within each of us. The moments when we choose presence over distraction, kindness over cynicism, courage over fear. The moments when we step outside the narrow boundaries of "me" and glimpse the vastness of "we." These are small, sometimes fleeting — but like acorns, they hold the potential to grow into forests.

The challenge, however, is that these seeds are fragile. Fear grows faster than love. Division spreads quicker than unity. Cynicism can choke hope before it has a chance to bloom. And yet history reminds us that seeds dormant for centuries can one day transform entire civilizations. The dream of equality lay buried for generations before abolitionists and suffragists gave it voice. The vision of nonviolence seemed powerless until Gandhi and Martin Luther King Jr. proved otherwise.

So it is now. The seeds of the New Human are present — in science, in spirit, in acts of ordinary courage. They do not yet dominate the landscape, but they are here, waiting to be nurtured. The question is not whether they exist, but whether we will water them with our attention and care. Will we let them wither under the weight of old fears? Or will we cultivate them into a garden strong enough to transform the soil of our collective life?

Every oak begins as an acorn. Every revolution begins small. The future of humanity depends on whether we recognize the seeds already at our feet.

CHAPTER 3 – REVOLUTION OF CONSCIOUSNESS

Every revolution has its battlefield. In the past, wars of change were waged on the streets, in factories, or on distant fields where empires clashed. But the battlefield of the New Human Revolution is not a place we can see on a map. It lies within us, in the invisible terrain of the human mind.

For centuries, humanity has tried to change the outer world without transforming its inner one. New governments replaced old ones, but often the hunger for power remained. Industrial advances multiplied wealth, but greed and inequality persisted. Even movements for freedom and justice sometimes fell into cycles of resentment and domination. The pattern repeated because the lens through which we perceived reality — consciousness itself — remained largely unchanged.

Consciousness is the foundation of everything we create. A mind rooted in fear imagines enemies everywhere. A mind obsessed with scarcity designs economies of hoarding and exploitation. A mind convinced of separation erects walls and hierarchies, dividing humanity into "us" and "them." Unless that lens shifts, even the most well-intentioned reforms risk reproducing the same old story in new forms.

This is why the New Human Revolution insists on beginning within. Change the inner, and the outer will follow. At first, this sounds poetic, even naïve. But look closer, and it reveals itself as a practical truth. When one individual learns to pause before reacting in anger, they break a cycle of violence. When a leader practices empathy instead of domination, an entire workplace begins to change. When communities cultivate trust, they withstand crises with resilience. These transformations begin in consciousness but ripple outward into society.

Examples abound. In prisons across the world, programs introducing mindfulness and meditation have reduced violence among inmates, offering glimpses of dignity and redemption where despair once ruled. In schools, children who practice simple breathing exercises are calmer, more focused, and more compassionate toward classmates. In corporations, leaders trained in mindful awareness are learning to guide teams with presence rather than pressure, shifting toxic cultures into spaces of creativity and trust.

Great spiritual teachers understood this long before neuroscience confirmed it. The Buddha spoke of awakening not as belief but as perception — to see the world without distortion. Jesus described the Kingdom of God not as a distant paradise but as something "within you." Sufi poets celebrated dissolving the ego into love, while Indigenous shamans taught that every stone, tree, and river was alive with spirit. Across cultures, the teaching was the same: liberation begins not by rearranging the world but by transforming how we see it.

Today, science affirms what sages have always known. Neuroscientists track how meditation rewires the brain toward empathy and compassion. Psychologists demonstrate how gratitude can shift perception from lack to abundance. Sociologists observe how communities rooted in cooperation and trust thrive even amid hardship. Far from mystical fantasy, the revolution of consciousness is grounded in observable fact: how we think and feel shapes the world we build.

And yet, this revolution is not easy. The human ego clings to old patterns with remarkable tenacity. It prefers certainty, even when certainty breeds suffering. It thrives on "us versus them," for it fears the dissolving of boundaries. To awaken is to risk letting go of familiar identities — to see ourselves not only as individuals but as participants in a larger whole. This requires courage, because it unsettles the very foundations of who we think we are.

But when consciousness shifts, the impossible becomes possible. Nations divided by conflict begin to imagine peace. Communities torn by prejudice begin to see one another as kin. Individuals once consumed by fear discover a well of resilience they never knew they possessed. A change of mind, multiplied across millions, becomes a change of world.

This is the heart of the New Human Revolution. It is not therapy for a select few; it is survival for the species. Without it, we risk repeating history's cycles until collapse. With it, we create the possibility of a world that does not yet exist — one guided not by fear, but by awareness, presence, and love.

The battlefield of this revolution is within us. The victory will not be measured in captured cities or toppled governments, but in awakened minds and liberated hearts. From there, everything else will follow.

CHAPTER 4 – TECHNOLOGY AND SPIRIT: ALLIES, NOT ENEMIES

Every age of humanity has been defined by its tools. The bow and arrow allowed hunters to feed their families and defend their tribes. The plow transformed soil into surplus harvests, supporting cities and civilizations. The printing press spread knowledge across continents, reshaping culture and religion. The steam engine shrank distances, the telegraph collapsed time, and the computer opened new dimensions of thought.

Today, we stand in the midst of yet another technological revolution. Artificial intelligence writes poetry and diagnoses illnesses. Biotechnologies edit the very code of life, raising the possibility of curing inherited diseases — and also of reshaping humanity itself. Satellites and digital networks encircle the Earth, weaving billions of people into an invisible web of constant contact. Virtual reality blurs the boundary between the physical and the imagined.

For many, this acceleration inspires awe and terror in equal measure. There is the thrill of possibility: cures for cancer, sustainable energy, knowledge at our fingertips. But there is also the anxiety of disruption: machines replacing workers, algorithms manipulating elections, technologies designed for profit eroding the very fabric of human attention. Some fear that in building such tools, we may lose touch with what makes us human.

The danger is real — but the danger does not lie in the tools themselves. Technology is a mirror. It reflects the consciousness of those who create and wield it. The same digital networks that spread conspiracy theories also carry messages of solidarity across borders. The same genetic technologies that could be used for vanity experiments could also eliminate devastating illnesses. The same artificial intelligence that threatens to flood the world with disinformation could also accelerate climate solutions and democratize education.

The old human story often used technology as a weapon of domination. The industrial age brought wealth, but also factories where children labored and landscapes blackened with soot. Nuclear science split the atom, producing both lifesaving medical imaging and weapons capable of ending civilization. The internet connected the globe, but also created platforms that profit from outrage and distraction. In each case, the spirit of exploitation shaped the use of invention.

The New Human Revolution insists that we can do better. It calls us to align our tools with wisdom rather than greed. Technology must become the servant of life, not its master.

Already, signs of this partnership are visible. In Kenya, mobile banking platforms have lifted millions out of poverty, allowing small farmers and entrepreneurs to access markets previously closed to them. In Bhutan, a country that measures "Gross National Happiness" rather than GDP, technology is carefully introduced to support well-being instead of unchecked growth. Virtual reality is being used in therapy to help veterans confront trauma in safe environments, proving that imagination, guided by compassion, can heal. Around the world, grassroots innovators are using solar panels and water purifiers to empower villages far from national grids, embodying the principle that progress can uplift without destroying.

And yet, there is also the temptation of speed. Inventions often arrive faster than our ethics can adapt. We design tools because we can, not because we should. We unleash technologies before pausing to ask whether they serve humanity's deeper purpose. The New Human Revolution demands a new discipline — to pause, to reflect, to bring questions of dignity, ecology, and spirit into the laboratories and boardrooms where the future is being designed.

What would it mean to let spirit guide technology? It would mean building platforms that foster dialogue instead of division, designing machines that extend human creativity rather than replace it, and developing economies where innovation is measured not only in profit but in contribution to life. It would mean teaching engineers and coders to see themselves not as neutral technicians, but as shapers of culture and custodians of humanity's future.

Without spirit, technology is a blind giant. Without technology, spirit risks remaining a whisper in the wind, unheard in the roar of modern life. But together, they can form a symphony — power and purpose woven as allies.

The task of our generation is not to slow invention but to deepen reflection. To ask, with each leap forward: *Does this serve life? Does this honor human dignity? Does this strengthen the web of existence we belong to?* If the answer is yes, then technology becomes not an enemy but an ally. If the answer is no, then the courage to say "not yet" or "not this way" becomes an act of revolutionary wisdom.

The New Human Revolution does not fear technology. It reclaims it. It insists that our tools can be shaped by compassion as well as ambition. If we succeed, the very machines that many fear will rob us of humanity may instead become the instruments through which humanity finally awakens.

CHAPTER 5 – FROM DIVISION TO UNITY

If there is one wound that has followed humanity through the ages, it is the wound of division. Again and again, we have defined ourselves by separation: tribe against tribe, nation against nation, class against class, race against race. We have drawn lines across land and across hearts, declaring who belongs and who does not. Entire civilizations have been built upon this logic of exclusion.

Division has a seductive power. It offers clarity in a complex world. It whispers: *We are the chosen, they are the outsiders. We are righteous, they are dangerous.* It builds walls both physical and invisible, giving us the illusion of safety while planting the seeds of perpetual conflict. From ancient wars between empires to the ideological battles of the modern world, the story has been the same: humanity splintered into camps, each convinced of its superiority, each blind to the shared truth beneath.

And yet, science and spirit alike testify to a deeper reality: we are one. Geneticists remind us that all humans are over 99 percent identical in DNA. Anthropologists trace every living person back to common ancestors in Africa. Physicists reveal that every atom in our bodies was forged in the heart of stars. Spiritual traditions, though diverse in language, echo the same truth — that life is an interconnected web, and that separation is illusion.

Still, unity is not uniformity. The New Human Revolution does not seek to erase difference, for difference is the source of richness. Just as a forest thrives through the diversity of trees, birds, and insects, humanity flourishes through the variety of its cultures, languages, and perspectives. Unity does not mean sameness. It means recognizing diversity as an expression of a shared essence, not as justification for superiority or oppression.

The old story of division is visible everywhere in our history. Colonialism carved artificial borders across continents, dividing people who had once lived in harmony. Apartheid in South Africa enforced separation with brutal laws, sowing decades of trauma.

Civil wars tore apart neighbors who had shared the same land for generations. Even today, politics in many nations thrives on division, fueling fear of "the other" to secure power.

Yet examples of unity breaking through division are just as powerful. After apartheid ended, South Africa chose not revenge but reconciliation, creating the Truth and Reconciliation Commission — an imperfect but courageous attempt to heal through acknowledgment rather than denial. In Northern Ireland, decades of sectarian violence began to yield to dialogue, proving that even centuries of enmity can soften when people dare to see each other's humanity. In Rwanda, survivors and perpetrators of genocide sit together in reconciliation villages, demonstrating that forgiveness, however painful, is possible.

Unity also reveals itself in moments of crisis. When earthquakes strike or floods destroy, people rush to help strangers, not stopping to ask about skin color, creed, or nationality. When global movements like *Black Lives Matter*, *Me Too*, *Water is Life*, or *Fridays for Future* rise, they remind us that injustice against one is injustice against all, and that the planet's fate binds us beyond borders.

But unity is not only political or social. It is also deeply personal. The divisions we see in the world mirror the divisions we carry within ourselves — between reason and emotion, ambition and values, who we are and who we pretend to be. To heal outer fractures, we must first heal the inner ones. The New Human learns to live as a bridge, integrating the parts of self that once felt fragmented. From that wholeness flows the ability to recognize the wholeness of others.

To move from division to unity requires courage. It asks us to risk vulnerability, to listen to stories that unsettle us, to sit with people whose perspectives challenge our own. It asks us to release the false safety of walls and discover the deeper safety of connection. And it asks us to imagine communities, nations, and economies organized not around competition but around belonging.

The New Human Revolution envisions politics rooted in stewardship rather than conquest, economies designed for circulation rather than hoarding, and communities defined not by survival but by celebration. This is not naïve dreaming; it is already being lived in small pockets of the world. Cooperatives where workers share profits. Cities redesigning themselves for inclusion and sustainability. Movements that cross racial, cultural, and religious lines to protect the Earth and one another.

Division has been the story we inherited. Unity is the story waiting to be written. The pen is in our hands. The question is whether we will continue scribbling in the margins of separation, or whether we will write a chapter worthy of the future.

CHAPTER 6 – HEALING THE PLANET, HEALING OURSELVES

The Earth has always been our silent companion. She has carried us through ice ages and droughts, earthquakes and storms. She has given us everything: the air in our lungs, the water in our veins, the soil that sustains our food, the forests that breathe for us, the oceans that cradle the web of life. And yet, in our pursuit of mastery, we have treated her less like a mother and more like a quarry.

For centuries, humanity believed the Earth to be limitless. Forests seemed endless, oceans appeared inexhaustible, and skies looked infinite. We took and took, mistaking generosity for abundance without end. But now the illusion is shattered. The forests shrink, the coral reefs bleach, the polar ice melts. We watch as entire species vanish before our eyes, as fires rage hotter, floods rise higher, storms strike harder. What once seemed infinite reveals itself as fragile.

And here lies a profound truth: our relationship with the Earth is a mirror of our relationship with ourselves. The exploitation of rivers, mountains, and forests reflects the exploitation of our own bodies and communities. The disconnection from soil and seasons mirrors the disconnection from our own hearts. To heal the Earth is to heal ourselves; to neglect the Earth is to wound our own future.

Science affirms what Indigenous wisdom has always taught. Time in nature heals us. Children who play among trees show stronger cognitive development. Patients recover faster when they can see green spaces from hospital windows. The Japanese practice of *shinrin-yoku*, or "forest bathing," has been shown to lower blood pressure, strengthen immunity, and reduce stress. The Earth is not just scenery; she is medicine. And the reverse is also true: when we heal her, we restore the systems that sustain life itself.

Across the world, signs of ecological healing are emerging. In Costa Rica, decades of deforestation were reversed through deliberate conservation and reforestation policies, turning barren hillsides back into lush forests alive with birdsong. In Kenya, the

Green Belt Movement, led by Wangari Maathai, mobilized women to plant millions of trees, healing landscapes while empowering communities. In urban centers like Singapore, rooftop gardens, vertical farms, and green corridors show that even cities can be designed as living ecosystems. Each of these efforts proves that restoration is not only possible but transformative.

The New Human Revolution sees the Earth not as property, but as kin. This changes the very foundations of how we live. It shifts economies from linear extraction to circular renewal. It reframes success not as endless growth but as balance and regeneration. It reawakens joy in simplicity — in walking rather than consuming, in community rather than accumulation, in harmony rather than conquest.

But healing is not only structural; it is deeply personal. When we touch the soil, we remember that we, too, are Earth. When we breathe the air, we remember that we, too, are sky. When we protect rivers, we protect the lifeblood that courses through our own veins. Healing the planet and healing ourselves are not two separate tasks; they are the same work seen from two angles.

Of course, the challenge is immense. The scale of ecological crisis can overwhelm even the bravest hearts. But history shows that collective courage begins with small acts. A community garden in a neglected neighborhood. A family choosing renewable energy. A group of citizens defending a forest from destruction. None of these alone will heal the Earth, but together — multiplied and sustained — they weave the fabric of a new future.

The Earth is not waiting for us to save her. She is inviting us to remember her — and in doing so, to remember ourselves.

In saving her, we save ourselves.

CHAPTER 7 – THE COURAGE TO CREATE

Every revolution needs courage. In the past, courage often meant standing on a battlefield, facing prison for truth, or risking life in defiance of tyranny. But the New Human Revolution calls for a different kind of bravery — not only the courage to resist, but the courage to create.

Creation is always an act of risk. To create is to bring into being something that did not exist before — a thought, a work of art, a movement, a way of life. Creation steps into the unknown, knowing there may be failure, ridicule, or misunderstanding. And yet, creation is at the very heart of what it means to be human. We are not merely consumers or survivors; we are storytellers, builders, healers, dreamers.

For too long, creativity has been treated as the domain of the gifted few — artists, musicians, inventors. But creation is the birthright of everyone. A farmer planting a new kind of crop in depleted soil is creating. A teacher who designs a lesson that awakens curiosity in her students is creating. A mother who sings a lullaby passed down through generations is creating. Creation is not limited to art; it is the act of shaping the world with imagination and love.

Why is creation revolutionary? Because systems of the old story thrive on passivity. They want us to consume, not to create; to obey, not to imagine. A passive citizen is easier to manipulate, a passive worker easier to exploit, a passive soul easier to forget. But when individuals awaken their creative power, they break the spell of helplessness. They realize they are not simply products of history but authors of it.

History is full of such courage. Vincent van Gogh painted against the ridicule of his contemporaries, never knowing that his work would one day inspire millions. Rosa Parks refused to surrender her bus seat, an act of defiance that became a spark of creation for the civil rights movement. Malala Yousafzai, still a child, chose to speak of education as a universal right even when her voice was threatened with silence. Each act of courage was also an act of creation — of a new possibility, a new world.

Creation can be bold and sweeping, or small and quiet. It can be the scientist daring to propose a solution no one believed possible, or the teenager painting a mural of hope on a cracked city wall. It can be a village rebuilding after a disaster with new ways of living, or an inventor designing technologies that heal rather than harm. Creation is not about scale, but about spirit.

Yet courage is needed because creation is fragile. The first attempts are clumsy. Early drafts fail. Society often resists what it cannot yet imagine. The courage to create is the courage to persist — to see failure not as defeat but as compost for future growth. The story of Thomas Edison's thousands of "failed" experiments is not one of failure but of perseverance. Every misstep became fertilizer for the eventual light bulb. So it is with all creation: what falters today becomes the soil of tomorrow's breakthroughs.

Creation is also defiance. To create beauty in the face of destruction is to declare that despair will not have the final word. To imagine new systems in the face of oppression is to insist that possibility is stronger than power. To bring forth life where others see only death is to proclaim that hope is alive.

And courage is contagious. When one person dares to create, others are emboldened to try. A culture of creation replaces a culture of consumption. Communities of makers replace communities of spectators. This is how revolutions endure — not only by tearing down the old but by building the new.

The New Human Revolution is not only about healing or awakening; it is about daring to imagine what has never been before — and then, trembling but resolute, stepping forward to bring it into being.

CHAPTER 8 – LIVING THE NEW HUMAN REVOLUTION

Revolutions are often spoken of in the past tense, as if they were storms that swept through history and left their mark. But the New Human Revolution is not a storm to wait for or a memory to recall; it is a way of living, a practice woven into the fabric of daily life. It belongs not only to great leaders or world-shaking events, but to the ordinary choices of ordinary people.

The temptation is to imagine revolutions as dramatic — banners raised, crowds assembled, declarations made. But the true work of the New Human Revolution is quieter. It is in the way a community decides to share food with the hungry. It is in the way a company chooses sustainability over profit at any cost. It is in the way an individual pauses before reacting in anger and instead responds with understanding. Revolutions do not always arrive with noise; sometimes they arrive with stillness.

To live this revolution is to embody the values it proclaims. It is to recognize that mindfulness is not a luxury but a necessity in a world addicted to distraction. It is to practice gratitude not as sentimentality but as an act of resistance against the culture of scarcity. It is to treat compassion not as weakness but as a radical force that reshapes relationships, workplaces, and communities.

But living the revolution also means reshaping the systems we inhabit. Education cannot remain confined to memorizing facts and passing tests; it must cultivate wisdom, empathy, and creativity. Work cannot be defined only by profit; it must contribute meaning and service to life. Governance must evolve from ruling by fear to guiding with stewardship, from defending divisions to nurturing unity. These systemic transformations may sound immense, but they begin in small decisions, repeated daily, until they take root as culture.

Communities of practice are crucial. Awakening does not happen in isolation. Just as forests thrive through networks of roots beneath the soil, humans flourish when bound together in communities of care and accountability. Spiritual circles, creative groups, and ecological cooperatives — all are expressions of the New Human Revolution in motion. Alone, we may falter. Together, we endure.

This way of living is not an escape from crisis but a response to it. The old human story reacts with fear and violence when threatened. The new human responds with presence, creativity, and resilience. The difference may seem small — one person breathing before speaking, one community choosing dialogue over conflict — but multiplied across millions, it becomes the difference between collapse and renewal.

The New Human Revolution is not a dream for tomorrow; it is an invitation for today. It is in this breath, in this act, in this step. Every gesture of kindness, every moment of awareness, every choice for creation over consumption is revolutionary. To live this way is to stop waiting for change and to begin being the change.

CONCLUSION – THE BIRTH OF A NEW HUMANITY

Every birth is both a struggle and a miracle. The New Human Revolution is no different. We are living through contractions of history — the old story breaking down, the new struggling to emerge. The pain is real: wars flare, ecosystems collapse, inequalities widen, fear multiplies. Yet within the pain, something astonishing is being born.

The old human story of fear, scarcity, and domination has brought us far, but it cannot carry us further. It has given us power without wisdom, wealth without equity, progress without peace. It has fractured our relationship with one another and with the Earth. But hidden within its failures are seeds of transformation — seeds of unity, compassion, creativity, and awakening.

The New Human is not a distant utopia or a flawless ideal. The New Human is us — ordinary people choosing to live differently. They are the healer who brings ancient wisdom into modern medicine. They are the young activist planting trees where forests were destroyed. They are the neighbor who refuses to let hatred dictate the future of their community. They are each of us, when we dare to see ourselves not as separate fragments but as participants in a living whole.

The birth of a new humanity will not be announced by trumpets or decrees. It will be seen in the way we heal the soil and heal our hearts. In the way we raise children to love rather than fear. In the way we build technologies guided by spirit rather than greed. In the way we learn to live as stewards, not masters.

If you are reading these words, you are already part of this birth. The revolution does not wait for permission. It does not belong only to leaders or heroes. It begins in the choices we make, in the lives we live, in the courage we embody.

One day, generations may look back and say: *This was the turning point. This was the dawn of a new humanity. Here, the old story ended, and the new began.*

The mirror of history is before us once again. It asks a simple question: *Who will you choose to be?*

The New Human Revolution has begun. And its birth is not out there, but here. Not someday, but today. Not in someone else, but in you.

ABOUT THE AUTHOR

Dr. W. Koros writes with a gentle yet powerful voice, guiding readers toward inner strength, humility, and self-discovery. His books inspire people to pause, reflect, and uncover the quiet wisdom already within them.